C · A · N · A · D · A

Romancing the Land

Lorraine Monk

Poetry by Miriam Waddington

KEY PORTER BOOKS

The publisher gratefully acknowledges the assistance
of the Canada Council and the Ontario Arts Council.

96 97 98 99 6 5 4 3 2 1

Canadian Cataloguing in Publication Data

Waddington, Miriam, 1917–
    Romancing the land

ISBN 1-55013-756-5

1. Canada – Poetry, 2. Canada – Pictorial works.
I. Monk, Lorraine. II. Title.

PS8545.A44R6 1996 C811'.54 C95-932959-5
PR9199.3.W3R6 1996

Key Porter Books Limited
70 the Esplanade
Toronto, Ontario
Canada M5E 1R2

Printed in Canada by Herzig Somerville Limited
Bound in Canada by York Bookbinders Inc.

The Photographers

Irwin Barrett	Michael Gillan	David Nunuk	John Sylvester
Daryl Benson	Victoria Hurst	Freeman Patterson	Peter Van Rhijn
Ralph Brunner	Rolf Kraiker	Gordon Petersen	Lisa Van Stygren
Harry W. Cartner	Lori Labatt	Steve Short	Ron Watts
David Chapman	Patricia Langer	Alan Sirulnikoff	Darwin Wiggett

Dedicated to the Romantic in all of us

In many ways, countries are like people. They need to be told, passionately and at regular intervals, how much we love them. How much we care. How important they are to the fabric of our lives.

Sometimes, we have to be on the brink of losing something, before we open our eyes, and our hearts, to what we might have let slip away. And so it seemed the time had come to speak about our love for Canada. To reaffirm our commitment to the land that defines us as Canadians.

Time to wake up and smell the wildflowers – the dense forests – the oceans that wash our shores – the pungent perfume of our wilderness places – the bountiful earth that stretches from sea to sea to sea. To embrace all the things we hold dear. A time to renew our faith in ourselves and in our country.

Now is the time to remember the wise words of our great writer and historian, Bruce Hutchison:

"We must look to the land and its secret cargo, if we are to learn the meaning of the nation . . . for the land, its abundance and its splendour, has always held the nation together."

And so we have compiled some of the most beautiful images ever taken with some of the most lyrical poetry ever written in a tender, loving letter to the place we call home.

Lorraine Monk

Let this be my poem

to you

you

you

you

only you.

PLATE 1

Lovers tread the waters
lovers go
in all the seasons
where the waters flow.

PLATE 2

We leap over rainbows
fly across winds
we are bewitched.

PLATE 3

*L*et's fly
be blue as air
fall off the world
weightless.

PLATE 4

 *am about to turn*
a million glittering cartwheels
in milky outer skies.

PLATE 5

his bubble of blue
swelling the vaulted sky
contains us.

PLATE 6

 sighing caress
in the sea green
sunlight.

PLATE 7

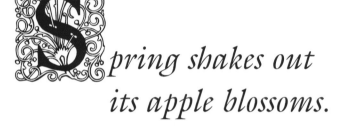

**S**pring shakes out
its apple blossoms.

PLATE 8

The coloured net of spring
was spread over the ocean
of our love.

PLATE 9

When I step out
and feel the green world
its concave walls must cup
my summer coming and curving
hold me beyond all geography
in a transparent place.

PLATE 10

Quiet and slow as a tide
over a smooth beach
with hardly a ripple to show
the sharp rocks of longing
buried seven fathoms below
consciousness.

PLATE 11

e hung
in the transparent bell
of summer.

PLATE 12

 *am still as a bird*
in a world entranced.

PLATE 13

hrough trees of space
distance leans in closer.

PLATE 14

Lying on our backs
our eyes fly up
higher than kites
clouds winds
higher than stars.

PLATE 15

Angels with red lanterns
hovered over us
their wings brushed us
with silence.

PLATE 16

nto the deep mountain of morning
now I stride holding my heart
a folded bird inside my hand.

PLATE 17

 become the legend of the earth
asleep in the stillness of earth.

PLATE 18

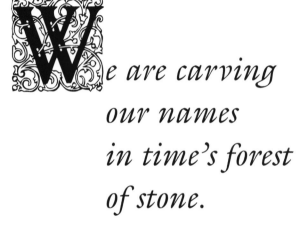

We are carving
our names
in time's forest
of stone.

PLATE 19

Love
remember me
as I do
you.

PLATE 20

**I** am asleep somewhere
above the wind love blind
I dream of pure nothing.

PLATE 21

Honied with
your gold of love
and love and still
again more love.

PLATE 22

*Six angels will I set
to watch the seed of your sleep.*

PLATE 23

e become the enchanted
land of ourselves.

PLATE 24

And the mind fills
with imagined love.

PLATE 25

*ow there is only
the whisper of grass.*

PLATE 26

*S*ometimes
it does no harm
to let mysteries
remain mysteries.

PLATE 27

*Singing and murmuring
the past is reminding
us to never forget.*

PLATE 28

he landscape sways
to the endless rhythms
of love.

PLATE 29

Photo Credits

Plate 1   Steve Short,
First Light,
Fraser Valley,
British Columbia

Plate 2   Lori Labatt,
Rainbow Falls,
near Schreiber,
Ontario

Plate 3   David Nunuk,
First Light,
Trail National Park,
Vancouver Island,
British Columbia

Plate 4   David Chapman,
Lake Weslemkoon,
east of Bancroft,
Ontario

Plate 5   Alan Sirulnikoff,
First Light,
west of Moose Jaw,
Saskatchewan

Plate 6   Ron Watts,
First Light,
Niagara Falls, Ontario

Plate 7   Lisa Van Stygren,
Nottawasaga Bay,
Northern Ontario

Plate 8   Freeman Patterson,
Long Reach,
New Brunswick

Plate 9   Patricia Langer,
Lake Mindemoya,
Manitoulin Island,
Northern Ontario

Plate 10   Ron Watts,
First Light,
Carmanah Rainforest,
British Columbia,

Plate 11   Lisa Van Stygren,
near Dorset, Ontario

Plate 12   Darwin Wiggett,
First Light,
Mount Kitchener,
Jasper National Park,
Alberta

Plate 13   Peter Van Rhijn,
Eagle Plains,
Northern Yukon

Plate 14   Rolf Kraiker,
Algoma Highlands,
Northern Ontario

Acknowledgements

Many people helped to make this book as beautiful as it is and I am deeply grateful to everyone of them.

Miriam Waddington agreed, with her usual grace, to permit me to use excerpts from her poetry to accompany the individual photographs. All of the selections are from her *Collected Poems*, published by Oxford University Press in 1986.

In my quest to find photographs that would capture the lyrical spirit of the land, I searched far and wide for the "perfect" picture. Once again I was reminded what a vast treasure trove of photographic talent we are heir to! As always, I am indebted to our wonderfully dedicated landscape photographers. They have shown us, through their unique and sensitive vision, the majesty and beauty of the place where we live. Every province and region of Canada is represented in this slender love letter to our country.

I would like to extend my warmest appreciation to Pierre Guevremont and his cordial staff at First Light photographic resource centre. In spite of my exhaustive and exhausting demands on their time and their patience, everyone was unfailingly kind and helpful.

The staff at Key Porter were supportive and caring. In particular, I would like to thank Jean Peters, who worked tirelessly to create a book that would present both the poetry and the photographs in a romantic and enchanting light!

Those brilliant technicians at Herzig Somerville have reproduced the photographs with their usual skill and magic, and I am, as so often in the past, delighted with their performance.

As always, I am indebted to my dear friend and colleague Nancy Smith. Without her generous support and encouragement, nothing I begin would ever get completed.

Lorraine Monk